D0065471

COMPILED BY
Dan Zadra with Katie Lambert

DESIGNED BY
Jenica Wilkie and Clarie Yam

COMPENDIUM™
PUBLISHING

live inspired.

ACKNOWLEDGEMENTS

These quotations were gathered lovingly but unscientifically over several years and, or contributed by many friends or acquaintances. Some arrived and survived in our files on scraps of paper and may therefore be imperfectly worded or attributed. To the authors, contributors and original sources, our thanks, and where appropriate, our apologies. —The Editors

WITH SPECIAL THANKS TO

Jason Aldrich, Gloria Austin, Gerry Baird, Jay Baird, Neil Beaton, Josie Bissett, Chris Dalke, Jim Darragh, Jennifer & Matt Ellison, Rob Estes, Michael Flynn, Jennifer Hurwitz, Heidi Jones, Carol Anne Kennedy, Erik Lee, Steve and Janet Potter & Family, Diane Roger, Drew Wilkie, Robert & Mary Anne Wilkie, Kristel Wills, Christy Wires, Heidi, Shale & Ever Yamada, Justi, Tote & Caden Yamada, Val Yamada, Kaz, Kristin, Kyle, Kendyl & Karli Yamada, Tai & Joy Yamada, Ann Zadra, August & Arline Zadra, Augie & Rosie Zadra.

CREDITS

Compiled by Dan Zadra with Katie Lambert
Designed by Jenica Wilkie & Clarie Yam

Printed in China

CHERISHED MESSAGES
OF HOPE, JOY, LOVE,
KINDNESS, AND COURAGE.

expect a miracle

Dr. Jo Blessing tells of an elderly patient who experienced a minor miracle in her life.

Despondent over the death of her only son, the old woman tidied up her little apartment one morning. On her night-stand she sprinkled out the sleeping pills. Then she trudged to her favorite place, a public park on the corner, where she sat alone, summoning the resolve she would need to end her life.

At noon something happened that changed her mind. Along came a man in an expensive-looking business suit. He was about the same age as her son, and he appeared to be in a hurry. For no particular reason, however, he suddenly stopped, smiled and stayed a few minutes to feed the pigeons with her. When he left, he touched her arm and said, "Good-bye–I can't remember when I've had a nicer time. Take good care of our little birds." He did not know that his kindness had restored her will to live.

Today, without even realizing it, you may be the answer to someone's prayers. Don't worry about whether you believe in miracles; just believe that your touch, your thoughtfulness, and your love really do work wonders in the lives of others.

Someone you know—a friend, neighbor, loved one, co-worker, or family member—may be hurting, doubting, wondering, or struggling. Give them this book; tell them that you're pulling for them, and that you believe in them. Tonight, call someone you care about. Tell them you miss them; tell them you're sorry. Arrange a visit. Make some lemonade or coffee. Take a walk. Enjoy the sun. Eat a popsicle. Feed the birds. Laugh, hug, cry. Invite a little miracle into your life. They are everywhere, and all around you.

Dan Zadra

GIVE THANKS
FOR UNKNOWN BLESSINGS
ALREADY ON THEIR WAY.

—NATIVE AMERICAN SAYING

The story's about you.

–HORACE

Do not wait for life.
Do not long for it. Be aware, always
and at every moment, that the miracle
is in the here and now.

–MARCEL PROUST

You are alive, and that is the only
place we need to be to start.

–CARRIE RAINEY

Time is a very precious gift—
so precious that it is only given to
us moment by moment.

—AMELIA BARR

Each instant is a place
we've never been.

—MARK STRAND

There is always one
unexpected moment in life when a
door opens to let the future in.

—GRAHAM GREENE

Think of the world
you carry within you.

–RAINER MARIA RILKE

You are not called to be
little canaries in a cage. You are
called to be eagles, and to fly
sun to sun, over continents.

–HENRY WARD BEECHER

Your aspirations
are your possibilities.

–SAMUEL JOHNSON

Life is a promise, fulfill it.

–MOTHER TERESA

You are the one and only you that
ever was, or ever will be. What you
are going to do with this miracle is
a question only you can answer.

–DAN ZADRA

Embrace your uniqueness.
Time is much too short to be
living someone else's life.

–KOBI YAMADA

There is nothing that
has to be done–there is
only someone to be.

–JACQUELYN SMALL

Everyone has a unique role to fill
in the world and is important in some
respect. Everyone, including and perhaps
especially you, is indispensable.

–JEAN RENOIR

Do not wish to be anything but what
you are, and to be that perfectly.

–ST. FRANCIS DE SALES

The great use of life is
to spend it for something
that will outlast it.

–WILLIAM JAMES

We are called upon to become
creators, to make the world new and
in that sense to bring something into
being which was not there before.

–JOHN ELOF BOODIN

Creativity is God's gift to you.
What you do with it is your gift to God.

–BOB MOAWAD

We become happier,
much happier, when we realize
that life is an opportunity rather
than an obligation.

–MARY AUGUSTINE

Today is your day and mine,
the only day we have, the day in which
we play our part. What our part may
signify in the great whole, we may not
understand, but we are here to play it,
and now is our time.

–DAVID STARR JORDAN

EVERY BLADE OF GRASS
HAS AN ANGEL THAT BENDS
OVER IT AND WHISPERS,
"GROW! GROW!"

–THE TALMUD

There came a time when the risk to
remain tight in a bud was more painful
than the risk it took to blossom.

–ANAÏS NIN

Why stay we on the earth unless to grow?

–ROBERT BROWNING

We must be willing to get rid of
the life we've planned, so as to have
the life that is waiting for us.

–JOSEPH CAMPBELL

It is only by risking from one hour
to another that we live at all.

–WILLIAM JAMES

Not to dream boldly may turn out
to be simply irresponsible.

–GEORGE LEONARD

Do not pray for tasks equal to your
powers; pray for powers equal to
your tasks.

–PHILLIPS BROOKS

Your dreams grow holy
put into action.

–ADELAIDE ANNE PROCTER

Somewhere someone is looking for
exactly what you have to offer.

–LOUISE L. HAY

Your work is to discover your work,
and then, with all your heart, to
give yourself to it.

–BUDDHA

Enthusiasm is a kind of
faith that has been set on fire.

–GEORGE MATTHEW ADAMS

The mind determines what's possible.
The soul surpasses it.

–PILAR COOLINTA

We never know how high we are,
Till we are asked to rise.

–EMILY DICKINSON

We were not sent into
this world to do anything into
which we cannot put our heart.

–JOHN RUSKIN

That is the simple secret.
Always take your heart to work.

–MERYL STREEP

Be faithful to that which exists
nowhere but in yourself.

–ANDRÉ GIDE

Just as there are no
little people or unimportant lives,
there is no insignificant work.

–ELENA BONNER

If I hadn't taken up painting,
I would have raised chickens.
It's all art.

–GRANDMA MOSES

It is possible, as you know, to make
a great painting on a small canvas.

–C.D. WARNER

It is often merely
for an excuse that we say
things are impossible.

–FRANÇOIS DE LA ROCHEFOUCAULD

It is not impossibilities which fill us
with the deepest despair, but possibilities
which we have failed to realize.

–ROBERT MALLET

Alas for those who never sing,
but die with all their music in them.

–OLIVER WENDELL HOLMES

I've learned that minor
miracles are fairly common in
the work-a-day world. Try long enough
and hard enough to do wonderful work
and, sure enough, you occasionally work
wonders.

–STEVEN SPIELBERG

When we do the best we can,
we never know what miracle is wrought
in our life, or in the life of another.

–HELEN KELLER

NOW YOU JUST BELIEVE.
THAT IS ALL YOU HAVE TO DO—
JUST BELIEVE.

–ADVICE FROM AN OLD OHIO FARMER

To me, faith means not worrying.

–JOHN DEWEY

Worry is a misuse
of the imagination.

–DAN ZADRA

There are only two emotions:
love, our natural inheritance,
and fear, an invention of our
minds which is illusory.

–GERALD JAMPOLSKY

Fear is faith that
it won't work out.

–SISTER MARY TRICKY

Trust your hopes.

–FATHER BILLINGS, S.J.

If you do not hope, you will not
find what is beyond your hopes.

–ST. CLEMENT OF ALEXANDRIA

Some things have to
be believed to be seen.

–RALPH HODGSON

The world was made round
so we would never be able to see
too far down the road.

–ISAK DINESEN

Patience! The windmill never
strays in search of the wind.

–ANDY J. SKLIVIS

Even if our efforts
seem for years to be producing
no results, one day a light that
is in exact proportion
will flood the soul.

–SIMONE WEIL

Let nothing dim
the light that shines from within.

–MAYA ANGELOU

You do build in darkness if
you have faith. But one day the
light returns and you discover that
you have become a fortress which
is impregnable to certain kinds of
trouble; you may even find yourself
needed and sought by others as a
beacon in their dark.

–OLGA ROSMANITH

What is to give light
must endure burning.

–VICTOR FRANKL

Nothing that is worth doing
can be achieved in our lifetime,
therefore we must be saved by hope.
Nothing which is true or beautiful
or good can make complete sense in
any immediate context of history,
therefore, we must be saved by faith.
And nothing we do, however virtuous,
can be accomplished alone, and
therefore, we must be saved by love.

–REINHOLD NIEBUHR

Fear knocked at the door.
Faith answered. No one was there.

–INSCRIPTION AT HIND'S HEAD INN, ENGLAND

THERE DOES,
IN FACT, APPEAR
TO BE A PLAN.

–ALBERT EINSTEIN

We talk about finding
God…as if He could get lost.

People see God every day,
they just don't recognize him.

–PEARL BAILEY

A coincidence may be God's way
of acting anonymously in your life.

–ANONYMOUS

The feeling remains that
God is on the journey, too.

–ST. TERESA OF AVILA

"For I know the plans
I have for you; plans to prosper
you and not to harm you, plans to
give you hope and a future."

–JEREMIAH 29:11

All I have seen
teaches me to trust the Creator
for all I have not seen.

–RALPH WALDO EMERSON

What you call holy,
we call love.

–LETTER TO A MISSIONARY FROM THE SENECA INDIANS

Each of us is loved,
as if there were only one of us.

–ST. AUGUSTINE

God loves you…
whether you like it or not.

–BUMPERSTICKER

I can't explain it.
All I know is that prayer works.

–NORMAN COUSINS

To those who believe,
no explanation is necessary;
to those who do not believe,
no explanation is possible.

–"THE SONG OF BERNADETTE"

They often pray best, who do not
know they are praying.

–UNKNOWN

God, give me guts.

–ELI MYGATT

God did not make us
to be eaten up by anxiety, but to
walk erect, free, unafraid in a world
where there is work to do, truth to
seek, love to give and win.

—JOSEPH FORT NEWTON

At night I turn
my problems over to God.
He's going to be up
all night anyway.

–MARY C. CROWLEY

Believe there is a great
power silently working all things
for good, behave yourself and
never mind the rest.

–BEATRIX POTTER

TO BELIEVE
IN IMMORTALITY IS ONE THING,
BUT FIRST BELIEVE IN LIFE.

–ROBERT LOUIS STEVENSON

You have to take time to live.
Living takes time.

–ELEANOR McMILLEN BROWN

Time is God's way of keeping
everything from happening all at once.

–UNKNOWN

Hold every moment sacred.
Give each its true and due fulfillment.

–THOMAS MANN

Earth's crammed with heaven.

–ELIZABETH BARRETT BROWNING

Life is the first gift, love is second,
and understanding third.

–MARGE PIERCY

We come. We go.
And in between we try
to understand.

–ROD STEIGER

In each of us
there is a little of all of us.

–GEORG CHRISTOPH LICHTENBERG

What lies behind us and what lies
before us are tiny matters compared
to what lies within us.

–RALPH WALDO EMERSON

I was never less
alone than while by myself.

–EDWARD GIBBON

The next message you need
is always right where you are.

–RAM DASS

When the student is ready,
the teacher will appear.

–ZEN SAYING

Teachers open the door,
but you must enter by yourself.

–CHINESE PROVERB

Some of life's greatest
lessons cannot be pried from books–
they must be experienced
in your bones.

–KOBI YAMADA

Somebody showed it to me
and I found it by myself.

–LEW WELCH

Nothing in life is more exciting
and rewarding than the sudden
flash of insight that leaves
you a changed person.

–ARTHUR GORDON

The delights of self-discovery
are always available.

I loaf and invite my soul.

–WALT WHITMAN

Who looks outside, dreams.
Who looks inside, awakes.

–CARL JUNG

One small step
up the mountain often widens
your horizon in all directions.

–E.H. GRIGGS

It is by tiny steps
that we ascend the stars.

–JACK LEEDSTROM

Raise your hopes and expectations
high enough, and you shall touch
wings with the divine.

–CELIA MORA

We're always trying to
move out of the darkness,
when all we have to do
is turn on the light.

–STEVE POTTER

When you come to the edge of
all the light you know, and must take a
step into the darkness of the unknown,
believe that one of two things will
happen. Either there will be something
solid for you to stand on–or you
will be taught how to fly.

–PATRICK OVERTON

ALWAYS KNOW IN YOUR
HEART THAT YOU ARE FAR
BIGGER THAN ANYTHING
THAT CAN HAPPEN TO YOU.

–DAN ZADRA

There are no mistakes, no coincidences.
All events are blessings given
to us to learn from.

–ELISABETH KUBLER-ROSS

Man needs difficulties;
they are necessary for health.

–CARL JUNG

"What is the heaviest burden?"
asked the child. "To have nothing to
carry," answered the old man.

–UNKNOWN

I've never been one who thought
the Lord should make life easy; I've just
asked Him to make me strong.

–EVA BOWRING

One should take children's
philosophy to heart. They do not
despise a bubble because it bursts.
They immediately set to work
to blow another one.

–KEYNOTE

Ah, if only you knew the peace
there is in an accepted sorrow.

–MADAME GUYON

I am more important
than my problems.

–JOSE FERRER

Out of every crisis comes
the chance to be reborn.

–NENA O'NEIL

Things fall apart so that things
can fall together.

–DAN ZADRA

When you're down
to nothing, remember that you
really do have the power to make
something out of nothing.

–DON WARD

When the friendly lights
go out, there is a light by
which the heart sees.

–OLGA ROSMANITH

Light tomorrow with today.

–ELIZABETH BARRETT BROWNING

LET US ALWAYS BE OPEN
TO THE MIRACLE OF THE
SECOND CHANCE.

–REVEREND DAVID STIERS

There will come a time when
you believe everything is finished.
That will be the beginning.

–LOUIS L'AMOUR

Never despair.

–HORACE

To deem any situation
impossible is to make it so.

–BERNARD DRUMMOND

Know in your heart that
all things are possible.

–DAN ZADRA

There is always, always,
always a way.

–ROBERT H. SCHULLER

Never give up on anybody.
Miracles happen every day.

–H. JACKSON BROWN

We couldn't conceive of a
miracle if none had ever happened.

–LIBBIE FUDIM

The idea that nothing is true except what
we comprehend is ridiculous.

–UNKNOWN

If I were absolutely certain
about all things, I would be fearful
of losing my way. But since everything
and anything are always possible, the
miraculous is always nearby and
wonders shall never, ever cease.

–ROBERT FULGHUM

What we need is
more people who specialize
in the impossible.

–THEODORE ROETHKE

The unexpected and the
incredible belong in this world.
Only then is life whole.

–CARL JUNG

When nothing is sure,
everything is possible.

—MARGARET DRABBLE

"But I can't believe impossible things,"
cried Alice. "Of course you can, child,"
responded the Queen. "Why, sometimes
I've believed six impossible things
before breakfast!"

–LEWIS CARROLL

There are only two ways to live your life.
One is as though nothing is a miracle.
The other is as though everything is a miracle.

–ALBERT EINSTEIN

The moment you move out of the way,
you make room for the miracle to take place.

–DR. BARBARA KING

Where there is great love
there are always miracles.

–WILLA CATHER

Just as angels are attracted to the light
of joy and kindness, so too are miracles
attracted to the lamp of faith and love.

–MARY AUGUSTINE

Someday all you'll have to light
the way will be a single ray of hope–
and that will be enough.

–KOBI YAMADA

A FRIEND
WALKS IN WHEN
THE WHOLE WORLD
WALKS OUT.

–UNKNOWN

People come into
your life for a reason, a season or
a lifetime. When you figure out which
it is, you know exactly what to do.

–UNKNOWN

We all go about
longing for kindred spirits.
To meet a stranger and, in the first
few seconds, to be able to guess
everything of any importance
about each other–well, this is
not a stranger at all.

–PILAR COOLINTA

"We two are friends"
tells everything.

–E.V. LUCAS

Oh, the comfort, the inexpressible
comfort of feeling safe with a person;
having neither to weigh thoughts nor to
measure words but to pour them all out,
just as it is, chaff and grain together,
knowing that a faithful hand will take
and sift them, keeping what is worth
keeping, and then, with the breath of
kindness, blow the rest away.

–GEORGE ELIOT

The most beautiful discovery
true friends make is that they can
grow separately without growing apart.

–ELISABETH FOLEY

Though love be deeper,
friendship is more wide.

–CORINNE ROOSEVELT ROBINSON

The truth is, friendship is every
bit as sacred and eternal as marriage.

–KATHERINE MANSFIELD

People love and appreciate others,
not just for who they are,
but for how they make us feel.

–IRWIN FREEDMAN

Friends are those rare people
who ask how we are, and then
wait to hear the answer.

–ED CUNNINGHAM

My lifetime listens to yours.

–MURIEL RUKEYSER

Dear George:
Remember, no man is a failure who
has friends. Thanks for the wings!
Love, Clarence the Angel

–"IT'S A WONDERFUL LIFE"

Whatever our souls are made of,
yours and mine are the same.

–EMILY BRONTË

Winter, spring, summer or fall
All you've got to do is call
And I'll be there, yes I will
You've got a friend.

–CAROLE KING

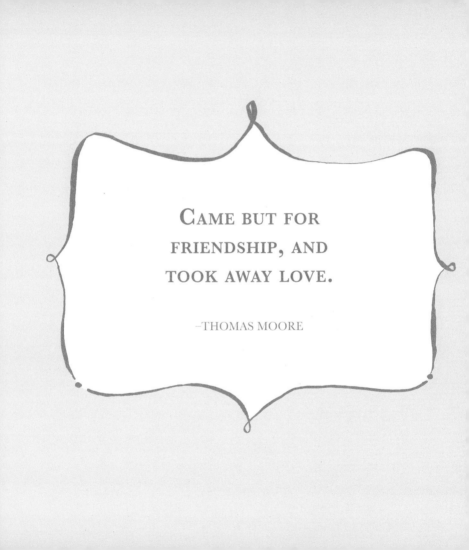

CAME BUT FOR
FRIENDSHIP, AND
TOOK AWAY LOVE.

–THOMAS MOORE

I give thee what could not be
heard, what has not been given before:
The beat of my heart I give.

–EDITH M. THOMAS

Two people in love.
Two people taking their
souls out for a dance.

–KOBI YAMADA

Then we sat on the edge
of the earth, with our feet dangling
over the side, and marveled that
we had found each other.

–ERIK DILLARD

There is no place love is not.

–HUGH PRATHER

And you, while you are a thousand miles away,
there are always two cups on my table.

–TANG DYNASTY POEM

The story of love is not important.
What is important is that one is capable of love.
It is perhaps the only glimpse we
are permitted of eternity.

–HELEN HAYES

Nice how love creates an
"us" without destroying a "me."

–LEO BUSCAGLIA

Love is a game
that two can play and
both can win.

–MICHAEL NOLAN

Love is the only game that is not
called on account of darkness.

–ANONYMOUS

Love is what you've
been through with somebody.

–JAMES THURBER

When people love each
other, an important kind of
giving is "giving in."

–LEO BUSCAGLIA

What a world this would be if
we just built bridges instead of walls.

–CARLOS RAMIREZ

Love comes unseen;
we only see it go.

–AUSTIN DOBSON

A heart can be broken,
but it will keep beating
just the same.

–FANNIE FLAGG

Loving can cost a lot;
not loving always costs more.

–MERLE SHAIN

There are only
four questions of value in life:
What is sacred? Of what is the
spirit made? What is worth living for?
What is worth dying for? The answer
to all four questions is the same:
Only love.

–"DON JUAN DEMARCO"

There is no
surprise more magical than
the surprise of being loved.

–CHARLES MORGAN

Love cures people–
both the ones who give it and
the ones who receive it.

–KARL A. MENNINGER

The conclusion is
always the same: love is the
most powerful and still the most
unknown energy of the world.

–PIERRE TEILHARD DE CHARDIN

It is safe to let the love in.
Love is your divine right.

–LOUISE L. HAY

To love is to receive
a glimpse of heaven.

–KAREN SUNDE

Never mind the past.
Let our scars fall in love.

–GALWAY KINNELL

Love seeks
not limits but outlets.

–ANONYMOUS

If we want a love message
to be heard, it has got to be sent out.
To keep a lamp burning, we have to
keep putting oil in it.

–MOTHER TERESA

Where there is no love,
put love–and you will find love.

SAINT JOHN OF THE CROSS

A BABY IS GOD'S
OPINION THAT THE
WORLD SHOULD
GO ON.

–CARL SANDBURG

"Where did I come from?"
the baby asked its mother.
She answered, half-crying, half-laughing,
and clasping the baby to her breast,
"You were hidden in my heart as
its desire, my darling. You were in the
dolls of all my childhood games.
In all my hopes and my loves, in my life,
in the life of my mother, and in her
mother before her, you have lived.
In the lap of the Eternal Spirit you
have been nursed and
anticipated for ages."

–RABINDRANATH TAGORE

It is no small thing when
children, who have so recently
come fresh from God, show
their love for us.

–KATHERINE MARSHALL

Children are not poets.
They are too busy being poems.

–UNKNOWN

Children are to be treated gently.
They are like snowflakes–unique,
but only here for awhile.

–DON WARD

A four-year-old boy gazed into the crib at his newborn baby sister and whispered to her, "Tell me again what God looks like–I'm starting to forget."

–ELIE WIEZCOFF

It is said, and it is true, that just before we are born, an angel puts a finger to our lips and says, "Hush, don't tell what you know." This is why we are born with a cleft on our upper lips and remembering nothing of where we came from.

–RODERICK MacLEISH

We only had one simple
rule in our home: Live harmlessly.

–SALLY BROWNE

What a father or mother says to
their children is not heard by the world,
but it will be heard by posterity.

–JEAN PAUL RICHTER

Help a child and
you help humanity.

–PHILLIPS BROOKS

In a child's lunchbox,
a mother's thought.

Children will not remember you
for the material things you provided, but
for the feeling that you cherished them.

We didn't have much,
but we sure had plenty.

Love, for Mama, was not
something she thought or talked about.
It was something she lived in action.
She showed us, as Mother Teresa has,
that love is found in sweeping a floor,
cleaning a sink, caring for someone ill,
or offering a comforting embrace.

–LEO BUSCAGLIA

Dad showed his love
by taking a wing for himself and
leaving the drumsticks for us.

–DON WARD

Even now,
twenty-one years after my
father died, not a week goes by
that I don't find myself thinking
I should call him.

–HERB GARDNER

Treasure each other in
the recognition that we do not know
how long we will have each other.

–JOSHUA LOTH LIEBMAN

THE BEST AND MOST
BEAUTIFUL THINGS IN THE
WORLD CANNOT BE SEEN OR
EVEN TOUCHED. THEY MUST
BE FELT WITH THE HEART.

–HELEN KELLER

The great lesson is that
the sacred is in the ordinary,
that it is to be found in one's
daily life, in one's neighbors, friends,
and family, in one's backyard.

–ABRAHAM MASLOW

It's good to have money and
the things money can buy,
but it's good, too, to check up once in
a while and make sure you haven't lost
the things money can't buy.

–GEORGE HORACE LORIMER

Just think how happy you'd be if
you lost everything and everyone
you have right now–and then,
somehow got them back again.

–KOBI YAMADA

Normal day, let me
be aware of the treasure you are.
Let me learn from you, love you,
bless you before you depart.
Let me not pass you by in quest of
some rare and perfect tomorrow.

–MARY JEAN IRION

Each of my days are miracles.
I won't waste my day;
I won't throw away a miracle.

–KELLEY VICSTROM

When will you know you have enough,
and what will you do then?

–BARBARA DE ANGELIS

I have never been a millionaire.
But I have enjoyed a crackling fire,
a glorious sunset, a walk with a friend
and a hug from a child. There are plenty
of life's tiny delights for all of us.

–JACK ANTHONY

Do not the most moving moments of
our lives find us all without words?

–MARCEL MARCEAU

I live on earth, where I am
surrounded by people who bless
me for "sneezing" and not for
living, singing or breathing.

–TOM HOPKINSON

The main thing is that we hear
and enjoy life's music everywhere.

–THEODOR FONTANE

Not everything that can be
counted counts, and not everything
that counts can be counted.

–ALBERT EINSTEIN

You are more–much more–
than what you have.

–DON WILSON

If you insist on measuring
yourself, place the tape around
your heart rather than your head.

–CAROL TRABELLE

Enough is a feast.

He has achieved success who has
gained the love of little children; who
has left the world better than he found it;
who has never lacked appreciation of
earth's beauty; who has looked for the best
in others and given them the best he had.

Where there is too much,
something is missing.

When the most
important things in our life
happen we quite often do not know,
at the moment, what is going on.

–C. S. LEWIS

When you have nothing left
but love, then for the first time you
become aware that love is enough.

–UNKNOWN

You are loved.
If so, what else matters?

–UNKNOWN

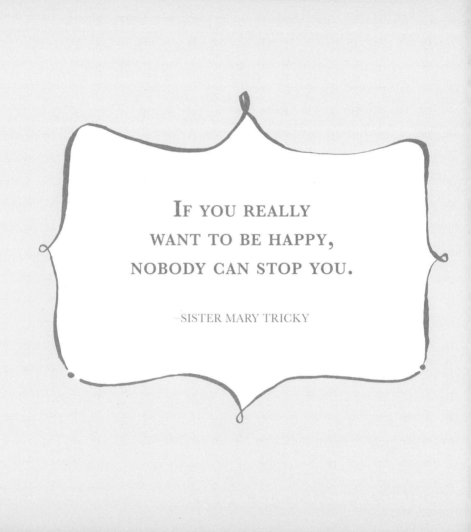

IF YOU REALLY
WANT TO BE HAPPY,
NOBODY CAN STOP YOU.

–SISTER MARY TRICKY

Joy is not in things;
it is in us.

I asked for all things,
that I might enjoy life.
I was given life, that I
might enjoy all things.

We are all happy if
we only knew it.

Learn to hold loosely
all that is not eternal.

–A.M. ROYDEN

Everything in life is most
fundamentally a gift. And you receive it
best, and you live it best, by holding it
with very open hands.

–LEO J. O'DONOVAN

How many cares one loses when
one decides not to be something,
but to be someone.

–COCO CHANEL

Be happy.
It is a way of being wise.

–COLETTE

If you laugh a lot, when you
get older your wrinkles will be
in the right places.

–ANDREW MASON

We don't stop laughing
because we grow old–we grow old
because we stop laughing.

–MICHAEL PRITCHARD

A laugh is
a smile that bursts.

–MARY H. WALDRIP

From there to here,
and here to there, funny things
are everywhere.

–DR. SEUSS

Dogs laugh, but they laugh
with their tails.

–MAX EASTMAN

Where is the yesterday
that worried you so?

I am an old man and
have known a great many
troubles, most of which have
never happened.

I am not afraid of tomorrow,
for I have seen yesterday and
I love today.

Birds sing after a storm;
why shouldn't people feel
as free to delight in whatever
sunlight remains to them?

–ROSE KENNEDY

If children with terminal cancer
can find peace, joy and
laughter in their day–and they do–
why don't we?

–DAN ZADRA

Resolved that I will take
each precious minute, and relish
all the joy within it.

–KATHLEEN RICE

HOW WONDERFUL IT IS
THAT NOBODY NEED
WAIT A SINGLE MOMENT
BEFORE STARTING TO
IMPROVE THE WORLD.

–ANNE FRANK

But where was I to start?
The world is so vast, I shall start
with the country I know best, my own.
But my country is so very large. I had
better start with my town. But my town,
too, is large. I had better start with my
street. No, my home. No, my family.
Never mind. I shall start with myself.

–ELIE WIESEL

Do not wait for leaders;
do it alone, person to person.

–MOTHER TERESA

The true meaning of life is to
plant trees under whose shade
you do not expect to sit.

–NELSON HENDERSON

Real generosity is doing
something nice for someone
who will never find out.

–FRANK A. CLARK

One must care about
a world one will never see.

–BERTRAND RUSSELL

The world will be saved
by one or two people.

–ANDRÉ GIDE

Do a deed of simple kindness,
Though its end you may not see,
It may reach, like widening ripples,
Down a long eternity.

–JOSEPH NORRIS

If something comes to life in others
because of you, then you have made
an approach to immortality.

–NORMAN COUSINS

The effect of one good-hearted
person is incalculable.

–ÓSCAR ARIAS

We must be the change
we wish to see in the world.

–MAHATMA GANDHI

When asked, "What can I do?"
I've found the answer frequently can
be found by rearranging the words
into the answer, "Do what I can."

–TEN MENTEN

A very important part
of the joy of living is
the joy of giving.

–WILLIAM BUCK

Caring is everything;
nothing matters but caring.

–FRIEDRICH VON HÜGEL

You have to reach out your hand,
that's what it's there for.

–MACKINLEE BARTON

Give what you have.
To someone it may be better
than you dare to think.

–HENRY WADSWORTH LONGFELLOW

What you are accomplishing
may seem like a drop in the ocean.
But if this drop were not in the
ocean, it would be missed.

–MOTHER TERESA

FEELINGS
ARE EVERYWHERE.
BE GENTLE.

–J. MASAI

Could a greater miracle take
place than for us to look through
each other's eyes for an instant?

—HENRY DAVID THOREAU

There is in each of us so much
goodness that if we could see its glow,
it would light the world.

—SAM FRIEND

If we could hear one another's
prayers it would relieve God
of a great burden.

—MICHAEL NOLAN

In our soup kitchens we
provide for people who are drifters.
They come for a meal, and some of them
don't eat at all. They just want to be
there in an atmosphere of peace and
tranquility. Most people don't just
want soup, they want contact where
they are appreciated, loved, feel wanted,
and find some peace in their hearts.
It's the personal touch that matters.

–SISTER DOLORES

If only all the hands that
reach could touch.

–MARY A. LOBERG

It takes courage for a
person to listen to his own
goodness and act on it.

–PABLO CASALS

You are not alone. We are all
connected. You could no more separate
yourself from humanity than a wave
could separate itself from the ocean
and still be a wave.

–GERALD JAMPOLSKY

Remember we all stumble,
every one of us. That's why it's
a comfort to go hand in hand.

–EMILY KIMBROUGH

We cannot live only
for ourselves. A thousand fibers
connect us with our fellow men;
and along these fibers, as sympathetic
threads, our actions run as causes,
and they come back as effects.

–HERMAN MELVILLE

108

If I just do my thing
and you do yours, we stand
in danger of losing each other
and ourselves. I must begin with myself,
true; but I must not end with myself.
The truth begins with two.

–WALTER TUBBS

We need
heart-to-heart
resuscitation.

–RAM DASS

Empathy is two hearts
pulling at one load.

–DAN ZADRA

Go ahead and cry,
I'll catch your tears.

–JILEEN RUSSELL

We can do no great things;
only small things with great love.

–MOTHER TERESA

It is not our toughness
that keeps us warm at night,
but our tenderness which makes
others want to keep us warm.

–HAROLD LYON

Don't forget to love yourself.

–SOREN KIERKEGAARD

WE ARE EACH OF US
ANGELS WITH ONLY ONE WING,
AND WE CAN ONLY FLY
BY EMBRACING EACH OTHER.

–LUCIANO DE CRESCENZO

God doesn't comfort us
to make us comfortable
but to make us comforters.

–UNKNOWN

As soon as healing takes place,
go out and heal somebody else.

–MAYA ANGELOU

People need your love
the most when they appear
to deserve it the least.

–JAMES HARRIGAN

Forgiveness is the finding again
of a lost possession.

–FRIEDRICH VON SCHILLER

There is a chord in every
human heart that has a sigh in it
if touched aright.

–OUIDA

Forgiveness is the answer to the
child's dream of a miracle, whereby what
is broken is made whole again.

–DAG HAMMARSKJÖLD

What value has
compassion if it does not take
its object in its arms.

–ANTOINE DE SAINT-EXUPÉRY

There is no such thing as
wasted affection.

–DAN ZADRA

Be not forgetful to comfort
strangers, for thereby some have
entertained angels unawares.

–HEBREWS 13:2

It is when we forget ourselves
that we do things that are most
likely to be remembered.

–UNKNOWN

Respect is what we owe.
Love is what we give.

–PHILIP JAMES BAILEY

Those whom we support
hold us up in life.

–MARIE VON EBNER-ESCHENBACH

It is an uncomfortable
doctrine which the true ethics
whisper in my ear. You are happy,
they say; therefore you are called
upon to give much.

–ALBERT SCHWEITZER

Those who give when they
are asked have waited too long.

–UNKNOWN

It is one of the most beautiful
compensations of this life that the more
you give away to others, the more
you get to keep for yourself.

–UNKNOWN

What I kept, I lost.
What I spent, I had.
What I gave, I have.

–HENRY BUCHER

God's arithmetic:
Happiness adds and multiplies as
you divide it with others.

–UNKNOWN

If we have no peace,
it is because we have forgotten
that we belong to each other.

–MOTHER TERESA

Giving never moves
in a straight line–it always
travels in circles.

–ROBERT SCHULLER

Have you had a
kindness shown? Pass it on.

–HENRY BURTON

Let no one ever come to you
without leaving better.

–MOTHER TERESA

NEVER PLACE A
PERIOD WHERE GOD
HAS PLACED A
COMMA.

–GRACIE ALLEN

Young. Old. Just words.

–GEORGE BURNS

There are trees that
seem to die at the end of autumn.
There are also the evergreens.

–GILBERT MAXWELL

What grows never grows old.

–NOAH BENSHEA

We are always the
same age inside.

–GERTRUDE STEIN

Those who love deeply
never grow old; they may die of
old age, but they die young.

–SIR ARTHUR WING PINERO

Parts of you are
still in unfinished business.

–"THE COLOR OF LIGHT"

Fire is seen in the eyes of
the young, but it is light we see
in the old man's eyes.

–VICTOR HUGO

I am delighted that even at my
great age ideas come to me, the pursuit of
which would require another lifetime.

–JOHANN VON GOETHE

To be alive, to be able to see, to walk,
to have houses, music, paintings–
it's all a miracle. I have adopted the technique
of living life from miracle to miracle.

–ARTHUR RUBINSTEIN

Come out of the
circle of time and into
the circle of love.

–RUMI

To live in hearts we
leave behind is not to die.

–THOMAS CAMPBELL

Your heart has brought
great joy to many. Those hearts
can never forget you.

–FLAVIA WEEDEN

It matters not how long
we live, but how.

A span of life is nothing.
But the man or woman who lives that
span, they are something. They can fill
that tiny span with meaning, so its
quality is immeasurable though its
quantity may be insignificant.

–CHAIM POTOK

The aim, if reached or not,
makes great the life.

–ROBERT BROWNING

Here is a test to find whether
your mission on earth is finished:
If you're alive, it isn't.

–RICHARD BACH

Attitude is more important than age.
Whether you're five or 105,
you have a lifetime ahead of you.

–DAN ZADRA

Sparrow, your message is clear:
it is not too late for my singing.

–TESS GALLAGHER

THE BEST IS YET TO BE.

·ROBERT BROWNING·

How simple it
is to see all the
worry in the
world cannot
control the future.
How simple it
is to see that we
can only be happy
now, and that
there will never
be a time when
it is not now.

–GERALD JAMPOLSKY

Other "Gift of Inspiration" books available:

Be Happy
**Remember to live, love,
laugh and learn**

Be the Difference

Because of You
Celebrating the Difference You Make

Brilliance
**Uncommon voices from
uncommon women**

Commitment to Excellence
Celebrating the Very Best

Diversity
Celebrating the Differences

Everyone Leads
**It takes each of us to make
a difference for all of us**

Expect Success
Our Commitment to Our Customer

Forever Remembered
A Gift for the Grieving Heart

I Believe In You
**To your heart, your dream, and
the difference you make**

Never Quit
**Inspiring Insights on Courage
& Commitment**

Reach for the Stars
Give up the good to go for the great

Team Works
Working Together Works

Thank You
**In appreciation of you, and
all that you do**

To Your Success
**Thoughts to Give Wings to
Your Work and Your Dreams**

Together We Can
**Celebrating the power of a
team and a dream**

Welcome Home
Celebrating the Best Place on Earth

What's Next
Creating the Future Now

Whatever It Takes
**A Journey into the Heart
of Human Achievement**

You've Got a Friend
**Thoughts to Celebrate the
Joy of Friendship**